WOMEN'S DAY POEM

AF525136

MEGHA YADAV

Copyright © Megha Yadav
All Rights Reserved.

This book has been self-published with all reasonable efforts taken to make the material error-free by the author. No part of this book shall be used, reproduced in any manner whatsoever without written permission from the author, except in the case of brief quotations embodied in critical articles and reviews.

The Author of this book is solely responsible and liable for its content including but not limited to the views, representations, descriptions, statements, information, opinions and references ["Content"]. The Content of this book shall not constitute or be construed or deemed to reflect the opinion or expression of the Publisher or Editor. Neither the Publisher nor Editor endorse or approve the Content of this book or guarantee the reliability, accuracy or completeness of the Content published herein and do not make any representations or warranties of any kind, express or implied, including but not limited to the implied warranties of merchantability, fitness for a particular purpose. The Publisher and Editor shall not be liable whatsoever for any errors, omissions, whether such errors or omissions result from negligence, accident, or any other cause or claims for loss or damages of any kind, including without limitation, indirect or consequential loss or damage arising out of use, inability to use, or about the reliability, accuracy or sufficiency of the information contained in this book.

Made with ♥ on the Notion Press Platform
www.notionpress.com

Contents

1. Strength

The power of women is a force to be reckoned with,
A strength that's deep and true,
They rise up from the ashes,
And their voices ring out anew.
From the fields to the boardrooms,
Their presence can't be denied,
Their stories are filled with courage,
And the battles that they've survived.
On this day we celebrate them,
And all that they have achieved,
The progress they've made for women,
And the rights they've bravely retrieved.
May we all stand together,
In solidarity and grace,
For the power of women is boundless,
And it shines on in every place.

Chapter2

Sisters United

Sisters united, hand in hand,
Together we rise, a mighty band,
With hearts that beat as one,
We stand up for what needs to be done.
In the face of adversity,
We hold each other up with tenacity,
We lift our voices, we make our choice,
To demand respect, to speak with one voice.
For every girl who dreams of more,
For every woman who's been ignored,
We rise to fight for equal rights,
For freedom, for dignity, for bright lights.
And so, on this day we celebrate,
All the women who dared to create,
A world where love and kindness reign,
Where every woman can thrive and gain.
Sisters united, we stand together,
Through every storm, in any weather,
For we know that when we unite,
Our power is unbreakable, our future bright.

3. For Maya

For Maya, who blazed a trail,
For every woman who will prevail,
For the ones who came before,
And for the ones who will open doors.
Maya Angelou, a voice so strong,
Her words will echo on and on,
A poet, writer, and civil rights leader,
Her courage, a legacy to always remember.
With words that stir the soul,
She spoke of struggle and of goal,
Of rising up and standing tall,
Of breaking barriers, and of shattering walls.
And so, on this day we honor her,
And all the women who dared to stir,
To raise their voices, to make a stand,
To fight for justice and for their land.
For Maya, and for every woman brave,
Who walks with strength and power, unafraid,
May we celebrate their spirit, their light,
And continue to champion their fight.

Chapter4

She stands with power in her stride,
Her head held high, with a fire inside.
She's unafraid to speak her mind,
To fight for her rights, for all womankind.
Her journey has been long and tough,
With obstacles that would be rough,
But she persevered and pushed ahead,
With hope and love that always led.
And now she stands as a symbol of strength,
A beacon of light, an inspiration at length,
For women everywhere who need to see,
That they too can rise up, and be truly free.
So on this day we honor her,
And all the women who came before,
We celebrate their strength and grace,
And the progress we've made in this place.

Chapter5

A woman's journey is one of grace,
Of strength, of love, and of fierce pace,
It's a journey of growth and of pain,
Of triumphs and victories, and a fight to sustain.
She walks a path that's all her own,
With courage and wisdom that's been honed,
Through hardships that test her spirit and will,
She finds a way to rise up still.
For she is a force to be reckoned with,
A warrior, a fighter, a queen, a myth,
With beauty that shines from deep within,
And a spirit that never gives in.
So on this day we honor her,
And every woman who dares to stir,
To fight for her dreams, and her destiny,
To be all that she's meant to be.
For a woman's journey is one of worth,
Of passion, of joy, and of rebirth,
And we celebrate the women who pave the way,
For a brighter tomorrow, a better day.

Chapter6

There is a warrior within every woman,
A fighter who rises up with strength unbroken,
She faces the challenges that come her way,
And battles through the toughest of days.
With each step she takes, she knows her worth,
And her determination inspires the earth,
For she is a force to be reckoned with,
A queen, a warrior, a goddess, a myth.
She holds her head high, with fierce grace,
And faces the world with unflinching face,
For she knows that every challenge she takes,
Is one step closer to the life she'll make.
So on this day we honor her,
And every woman who's dared to stir,
To awaken the warrior within,
And rise up with strength, and a fighting grin.
For a woman's power knows no bounds,
And her strength and courage will resound,
As she takes her place in the world today,
And fights for her rights, come what may.

Chapter7

There is a light within every woman,
A flame that burns with the power of a thousand suns,
It shines so bright, with a radiance so true,
And it can light up the world, with a strength that's anew.
It's a light that guides her through the darkest of days,
And illuminates the path to her destiny and ways,
For she knows that with each step she takes,
She'll be closer to her dreams, and her goals she'll make.
And so, she moves forward with fierce grace,
With the power of her light, and her courage in place,
For she knows that every obstacle she'll face,
Is just another chance, to rise up with grace.
And on this day, we celebrate her light,
And every woman who's shone so bright,
For it's with her power, and her fire within,
That she'll light up the world, and rise up to win.
For a woman's light knows no bounds,
And it shines with a brilliance, that astounds,
So let's celebrate her, and all she brings,
And let her light shine, in everything.

8. The Power of Sisterhood

There is a power in sisterhood,
A bond that cannot be misunderstood,
For when women come together as one,
Their power is greater than the sum.
With love and kindness as their guide,
They stand up tall, side by side,
For they know that when they unite,
Their power can overcome any fight.
And so, they rise up, with fierce grace,
Determined to make a positive change,
To fight for equal rights, and freedom for all,
And to break down barriers, that once stood tall.
For the power of sisterhood is strong,
And it's something that's been there all along,
For when women come together in solidarity,
Their power can move mountains, with tenacity.
And so, on this day, we celebrate,
All the women who've dared to create,
A world where sisterhood can thrive,
And where women can be truly alive.
For the power of sisterhood is a force to be reckoned,
And it's something that cannot be mistaken,

For when women stand together in unity,
Their power knows no limits, with its community.

9. Her Inner Strength

There's an inner strength in every woman,
A power that's mighty, and can move a mountain,
It's a strength that comes from deep within,
And it's the very essence of her being.
She carries it with her every day,
As she goes about her life, in her own way,
For she knows that with each challenge she takes,
Her inner strength will help her to overcome the stakes.
It's the strength of her spirit, and the power of her soul,
That keeps her moving forward, towards her goals,
And though the path may not always be clear,
Her inner strength will guide her, with no fear.
For she is a warrior, and a fighter, and a queen,
With a spirit that's fierce, and a heart that's keen,
And with her inner strength as her guide,
She'll face any challenge, with a fearless stride.
So on this day, we honor her,
And every woman who's dared to stir,
The inner strength that's deep inside,
And rise up, with grace, and her spirit as her guide.
For a woman's inner strength is a power so great,
And it's something that cannot be debated,
For with it, she can conquer anything,

And make her dreams, a reality, everything.

10. The Unstoppable orce

There's an unstoppable force in every woman,
A power that's fierce, and can move a mountain,
It's a force that's been there since the dawn of time,
And it's the very essence of her divine.
She carries it with her every day,
As she goes about her life, in her own way,
For she knows that with each step she takes,
Her unstoppable force will guide her, through any stakes.
It's the force of her spirit, and the power of her soul,
That keeps her moving forward, towards her goal,
And though the path may not always be easy,
Her unstoppable force will guide her, and never leave her queasy.
For she is a warrior, and a fighter, and a queen,
With a spirit that's fierce, and a heart that's keen,
And with her unstoppable force as her guide,
She'll face any challenge, with an unwavering stride.
So on this day, we honor her,
And every woman who's dared to stir,
The unstoppable force that's deep inside,
And rise up, with strength, and with her spirit as her guide.
For a woman's unstoppable force is a power so great,
And it's something that cannot be debated,

For with it, she can conquer anything,
And make her dreams, a reality, everything.

Chapter11

There's a beauty in every woman,
A light that shines from deep within,
It's a beauty that's more than skin deep,
And it's the very essence of her unique.
Her beauty is in her strength, and her grace,
In the way she moves, and the smile on her face,
It's in the kindness she shows, and the love she gives,
And in the way she lives her life, and how she lives.
For she is a reflection of all that is good,
And her beauty shines bright, like a star in the hood,
She's a symbol of hope, and of all that is right,
And her beauty is a beacon, that shines through the night.
So on this day, we honor her,
And every woman who's dared to stir,
The beauty that's deep inside,
And rise up, with pride, and with her spirit as her guide.
For a woman's beauty is a power so great,
And it's something that cannot be debated,
For with it, she can change the world,
And make it a better place, with her flag unfurled.

12. A Women's

Her worth is not determined by the clothes she wears,
Or the makeup on her face, or the style of her hair,
It's not about her size, or her weight, or her shape,
Or the way she moves, or the way she speaks.
Her worth is in the strength of her spirit,
In the power of her soul, and the depth of her wit,
It's in the way she loves, and the way she cares,
And in the way she faces life, with grace and with flare.
For she is a woman, strong and proud,
With a voice that's loud, and a heart that's vowed,
To make a difference, in the world she lives,
And to give of herself, and all that she gives.
So on this day, we honor her,
And every woman who's dared to stir,
The fire that's deep inside,
And rise up, with power, and with her spirit as her guide.
For a woman's worth is a power so great,
And it's something that cannot be debated,
For with it, she can change the world,
And make it a better place, with her flag unfurled.

Chapter13

She walks through life, with purpose and grace,
Leaving behind, a trail of her own unique trace,
For she is a woman, strong and bold,
And her legacy is something that will never grow old.
Her legacy is in the way she lives her life,
In the way she faces challenge, struggle, and strife,
It's in the way she loves, and the way she cares,
And in the way she gives of herself, and all that she shares.
For she is a force, to be reckoned with,
And her legacy will always be a beautiful myth,
Of a woman who stood tall, in the face of adversity,
And never gave up, on her dreams or her diversity.
So on this day, we honor her,
And every woman who's dared to stir,
The legacy that's deep inside,
And rise up, with courage, and with her spirit as her guide.
For a woman's legacy is a power so great,
And it's something that cannot be debated,
For with it, she can change the world,
And make it a better place, with her flag unfurled.

14. A Woman's Heart

In the heart of every woman,
There's a fire that burns so bright,
A passion that drives her forward,
And a spirit that takes flight.
It's a heart that's full of courage,
And a soul that's full of grace,
It's a heart that's always giving,
And a spirit that can't be replaced.
For a woman's heart is a force to be reckoned,
A power that can never be broken or second-guessed,
It's a heart that loves deeply,
And a soul that's endlessly blessed.
So on this day, we honor her,
And every woman who's dared to stir,
The fire that's deep inside,
And rise up, with passion, and with her spirit as her guide.
For a woman's heart is a power so great,
And it's something that cannot be debated,
For with it, she can change the world,
And make it a better place, with her flag unfurled.

15. She Rises

She rises up each morning, with the sun in her eyes,
With a heart full of hope, and a spirit that flies,
For she is a woman, strong and fierce,
And she faces each day, with a purpose so clear.
She rises up each morning, with the world on her back,
And she carries it with grace, without a single crack,
For she is a woman, brave and bold,
And she faces each challenge, with a story to be told.
She rises up each morning, with a fire in her heart,
With a love that's so strong, it can never be torn apart,
For she is a woman, wise and true,
And she lives her life, with a passion so new.
So on this day, we honor her,
And every woman who's dared to stir,
The fire that's deep inside,
And rise up, with power, and with her spirit as her guide.
For a woman's strength is a power so great,
And it's something that cannot be debated,
For with it, she can change the world,
And make it a better place, with her flag unfurled.

Chapter16

In the sound of a woman, there's a song that's so pure,
A melody that echoes, through every heart that's unsure,
For she is a woman, with a voice that's so strong,
And she sings her song, with a purpose that belongs.
She sings of love and hope, of dreams and desire,
Of a world that's so bright, it sets every soul on fire,
For she is a woman, with a heart that's so bold,
And she sings her song, with a story to be told.
She sings of the struggles, and the battles she's won,
Of the mountains she's climbed, and the wars she's begun,
For she is a woman, with a spirit that's so free,
And she sings her song, with a passion that can't be.
So on this day, we honor her,
And every woman who's dared to stir,
The sound that's deep inside,
And sing her song, with her spirit as her guide.
For a woman's song is a power so great,
And it's something that cannot be debated,
For with it, she can change the world,
And make it a better place, with her flag unfurled.

Chapter17

In the dance of a woman, there's a rhythm so sweet,
A movement that's graceful, with every step and beat,
For she is a woman, with a body that's strong,
And she dances her dance, with a spirit that belongs.
She dances of joy and laughter, of love and delight,
Of a world that's so colorful, it fills every sight,
For she is a woman, with a heart that's so free,
And she dances her dance, with a passion that can't be.
She dances of the struggles, and the battles she's won,
Of the mountains she's climbed, and the wars she's begun,
For she is a woman, with a spirit that's so bold,
And she dances her dance, with a story to be told.
So on this day, we honor her,
And every woman who's dared to stir,
The dance that's deep inside,
And move to her rhythm, with her spirit as her guide.
For a woman's dance is a power so great,
And it's something that cannot be debated,
For with it, she can change the world,
And make it a better place, with her flag unfurled.

Chapter18

In the light of a woman, there's a glow so bright,
A radiance that shines, even in the darkest night,
For she is a woman, with a soul that's so pure,
And she shines her light, with a purpose that endures.
She shines of love and kindness, of compassion and care,
Of a world that's so full, it's beyond compare,
For she is a woman, with a heart that's so giving,
And she shines her light, with a spirit that's so living.
She shines of the struggles, and the battles she's faced,
Of the mountains she's climbed, and the strength she's embraced,
For she is a woman, with a spirit that's so resilient,
And she shines her light, with a story that's brilliant.
So on this day, we honor her,
And every woman who's dared to stir,
The light that's deep inside,
And shine so bright, with her spirit as her guide.
For a woman's light is a power so great,
And it's something that cannot be debated,
For with it, she can change the world,
And make it a better place, with her flag unfurled.

9 798889 757061

Printed by Libri Plureos GmbH in Hamburg,
Germany